The Princess and the poo

by

Lara Fairy Love

Illustrations by Jenna Andreotti

AiMS

There for your mother
Here for you
Help us to be there for your daughters

Published by AIMS on behalf of Lara Fairy Love

Association for Improvements in the Maternity Services
Registered Charity number 1157845

www.aims.org.uk

ISBN 978-1-4716-2832-0

Printed in the Czech Republic by Printo

About AIMS

The Association for Improvements in the Maternity Services (AIMS) has been at the forefront of the childbirth movement since 1960. Run entirely by unpaid volunteers, it became a Registered Charity in 2014.

AIMS day-to-day work includes providing independent support and information about maternity choices and raising awareness of current research on childbirth and related issues. AIMS actively supports parents and healthcare professionals who recognise that, for the majority of women, birth is normal rather than a medical event. AIMS campaigns tirelessly on many issues covered by the Human Rights legislation.

Foreword from the AIMS Committee

You may be surprised that AIMS has chosen to support the publication of The Princess and the Poo — not our 'normal' kind of book! However, AIMS has never claimed to be mainstream and predictable so here is an unusual contribution to our range of books.

The Princess and the Poo is a delightful, insightful story for everyone, young and old, to understand the power of physiological birth. By educating and empowering our young people to know that childbirth can be free from fear and restriction and, in fact, be joyful and peaceful — we can pass on every woman's birthright through the generations!

The author Lara Fairy Love is an inspirational childbirth helper (her own words) and has the most incredible website www.fairydoula.co.uk.

Jenna Andreotti illustrated this book with alluring, colourful drawings bringing to a new generation the story of the Princess who lived happily ever after (sorry for ruining the end, but we think you could guess!).

We hope you enjoy this book and will pass it on to all the young people you know.

This book is dedicated to
all the children of the world
especially
Blue, Jemo, Jenny, Aaron,
Josephine, Miella
and Charlie.

~~~

For the purpose of creating
Beautiful Birth experiences,
World Peace and Global solidarity.
A portion of all proceeds are gifted
to the Holy work of
Little Miracles Foundation
(Josie & Billi Rose) and
Towards Tomorrow Together
(Mel & Finlay).

Once upon a time, out of time,

There was a princess called Rose.

She was a perfect princess,

From her head to her toes.

Princess Rose had a perfect mouth,

Perfect eyes, perfect ears, perfect nose,

Perfect hair, perfect skin, perfect front,

Perfect back, perfect top

And perfect belows.

Perfect Rose married a perfect prince

And he built her a perfect home.

A pink and perfect palace,

With gardens in to roam.

It had bedrooms and sewing rooms,

Kitchens and attics,

Lobbies and drawing rooms

And rooms to hang hats in.

A room for all activities

That a Princess should do...

So of course there was nowhere

For having a poo!

The Princess sat chewing

Her dinner one night,

Wondering what she could do

To resolve her bum plight.

And she couldn't ask Prince Charming

The way to the loo,

Because everyone knows

Perfect Princesses don't poo!

Just as she thought

Her bum would explode,

From a door in the wall

Came the end of a nose.

On the end of the nose

Was a little old crone,

Who beckoned the maid

To a porcelain throne.

The Princess rushed over

With her hands on her botty,

And quickly sat down

On the newly-found potty.

As a rush of relief

Came over young Rose,

She turned once again

To the crone with the nose.

The crone with her knitting

Was really engrossed.

Her long fingers and needles

Clicked as they crossed.

But then with a smile

She put her work down

And focused her will

On the girl in the gown.

"Poo", said the woman

With a smile in her eyes,

"Poo is the secret

We must no longer disguise!"

"My son built a palace

Of perfection, it's true,

But perfect for him,

Not perfect for you.

The use of your bottom

Is integral to all ladies,

For if you know how to poo...

You will know how to have babies!"

"Babies that are healthy,

Babies that love,

Babies that fit your body

Like a hand to a glove."

"I am old as you see,"

Said the crone with the nose,

"And the secrets I tell

Every woman could know."

" 'Could' but they don't,

Because perfect is easy

'Quicker', 'Convenient',

With no pains making you queasy.

They want doctors and beds,

And electronic ears

Charting their 'progress',

Creating their 'fears'."

"Your body is perfect,

Your body is real,

Your body knows what you need

If you're brave enough to feel!

The knowledge contained

In each little lady

Knows all of the moves

For birthing a baby!"

"Strength in your belly,

Strength in your thighs,

Strength in your baby,

Strength in your mind!"

"But why?" said the Princess,

"Why have the pain

When there is all this technology

To dampen my brain?"

The little old lady

Turned with a grin,

"There's no describing the power

That comes from within."

"As you deal with your pain

And face up to your fears,

The plain facts of the matter

Are abundantly clear."

"Your body is healthy,

Your body is good,

Your body knows how to give birth

The way that it should.

And every cell

That makes up your system

Is filled with generations

Of Birthing Mothers Wisdom!"

Sophies Wisdom Family Album

"But poo?" said the Princess,

"Is that really the key?

Cos poo bottoms and babies

All sounds too ickeee!"

"Laughter and Love

Are your two other powers,

With them as your guides

You will open up like flowers."

The Princess called Rose

Looked up to her friend,

Who showed her the fields

Of wild flowers without end.

Now armed with the knowledge,

That all women

Can claim as their own,

Rose went home to reclaim her throne.

So, Sophie she smiled

The smile of a Mother,

Who has passed on her Wisdom

From one to another.

And the very next year

When she gave birth to her baby,

Rose was attended by

Her Love, and the little old Lady.

A joyful time for all

As the baby came down,

No panic, no fear,

No screaming, no frowns,

The Baby all healthy,

And the Princess was too!

And all because she was

Brave enough

To learn how to poo!

So the Prince he was happy,

Because his love was so clever,

And Prince, Princess and Baby,

Lived happily ever after....

Forever!

Please let us know your views of this book by emailing:
feedback@aims.org.uk

Other AIMS publications can be ordered from the
AIMS website – www.aims.org.uk/shop

- Am I Allowed?
- Birth After Caesarean
- Birthing Your Baby: The Second Stage
- Birthing Your Placenta: The Third Stage
- Breech Birth – What are my options?
- Inducing Labour – Making Informed Decisions
- Group B Strep Explained
- Safety in Childbirth
- Caesarean Birth – Your Questions Answered

We are pleased to offer some of these books on Kindle. The link
to Amazon to purchase the kindle file is below each book cover
on the following page:
www.aims.org.uk/general/aims-kindle-publications

AİMS

There for your mother
Here for you
Help us to be there for your daughters

www.aims.org.uk
Twitter – @AIMS_online
Facebook – www.facebook.com/AIMSUK
Helpline 0300 365 0663
helpline@aims.org.uk